Animal 911
ENVIRONMENTAL THREATS

Poaching and Illegal Trade

NICOLE SHEA

Gareth Stevens
Publishing

Please visit our website, www.garethstevens.com
For a free color catalog of all our high-quality books,
call toll free 1-800-542-2595 or fax 1-877-542-2596.

Library of Congress Cataloging-in-Publication Data

Shea, Nicole.
Poaching and illegal trade / by Nicole Shea.
 p. cm. — (Animal 911: environmental threats)
Includes index.
ISBN 978-1-4339-9719-8 (pbk.)
ISBN 978-1-4339-9720-4 (6-pack)
ISBN 978-1-4339-9718-1 (library binding)
1. Poaching—Juvenile literature. I. Shea, Nicole, 1976- II. Title.
SK36.7 S47 2014
364.162—dc23

First Edition

Published in 2014 by
Gareth Stevens Publishing
111 East 14th Street, Suite 349
New York, NY 10003

© 2014 Gareth Stevens Publishing

Produced by Planman Technologies
Designed by Sandy Kent
Edited by Jon Bogart

Photo Credits: Cover: Mirekphoto/Dreamstime; Background: LeksusTuss/Shutterstock.com; Inside: Pg 4: Peter Betts/
Shutterstock.com; Pg 5: ©M. Krofel Wildlife/Alamy/IndiaPicture; Pg 6: ©Images of Africa Photobank/Alamy/IndiaPicture;
Pg 7: Cynthia Kidwell/Shutterstock.com; Pg 8: Jeff Banke/Shutterstock.com; Pg 9: Jamen Percy/Shutterstock.com; Pg 10:
©National Geographic Image Collection/Alamy/IndiaPicture; Pg 11: ©Gallo Images/Alamy/IndiaPicture; Pg 12: ©Aivar
Mikko/Alamy/IndiaPicture; Pg 13: ©Chad Ehlers/Alamy/IndiaPicture; Pg 14: ©Travel Pix/Alamy/IndiaPicture; Pg 15:
©Erich Haefele/Alamy/IndiaPicture; Pg 16: Charles Taylor/Shutterstock.com; Pg 17: ©Terry Whittaker/Alamy/IndiaPicture;
Pg 18: Food Collection/IndiaPicture; Pg 19: ©Steve Morgan/Alamy/IndiaPicture; Pg 20: ©Images of Africa Photobank/
Alamy/IndiaPicture; Pg 21: Critterbiz/Shutterstock.com; Pg 22: ©ZUMA Wire Service/Alamy/IndiaPicture; Pg 23: Hedrus/
Shutterstock.com; Pg 24: ©Matthew Oldfield Underwater Photography/Alamy/IndiaPicture; Pg 25: Bork/Shutterstock.
com; Pg 26: Ludmila Yilmaz/Shutterstock.com; Pg 27: ©Images of Africa Photobank/Alamy/IndiaPicture; Pg 28: Jonathan
Pledger/Shutterstock.com; Pg 29: l i g h t p o e t/Shutterstock.com; Pg 30: ©Gay Bumgarner/Alamy/IndiaPicture; Pg 31:
Karel Gallas/Shutterstock.com; Pg 32: National Geography/IndiaPicture; Pg 33: Angela Waye/Shutterstock.com; Pg 36:
Mogens Trolle/Shutterstock.com; Pg 37: Stephen McSweeny/Shutterstock.com; Pg 38: Irina Afonskaya/Shutterstock.com;
Pg 39: Tom Reichner/Shutterstock.com; Pg 40: Praisaeng/Shutterstock.com; Pg 41: Prasit Chansareekorn/Shutterstock.
com; Pg 42: ©Doug Houghton/Alamy/IndiaPicture; Pg 43: ©Steve Taylor ARPS/Alamy/IndiaPicture; Pg 44: Antonio
Abrignani/Shutterstock.com; Pg 45: ©Pete Titmuss/Alamy/IndiaPicture.

Artwork created by Planman Technologies: 34; 35.

Printed in the United States of America

CPSIA compliance information: Batch #CS13GS. For further information contact Gareth Stevens, New York,
New York at 1-800-542-2595.

Contents

Words in the glossary appear in **bold** type the first time they are used in the text.

What Is Poaching?

On the plains of Africa, there are few sights more amazing than a herd of elephants. Elephants are the largest land animals in the world. These giant creatures are proud and remind us of how great nature can be.

Imagine going to Africa, and instead of seeing elephants with legs like trees, their famous trunks, and their long ivory tusks, you see an elephant dead on the ground with its tusks torn out.

Or you see a rhinoceros wandering about in great pain because its horn has been cut off.

Who would do these things? **Poachers.** Poachers are people who hunt and kill animals illegally.

Healthy elephants are a sign of a thriving environment. They are, however, hard to protect.

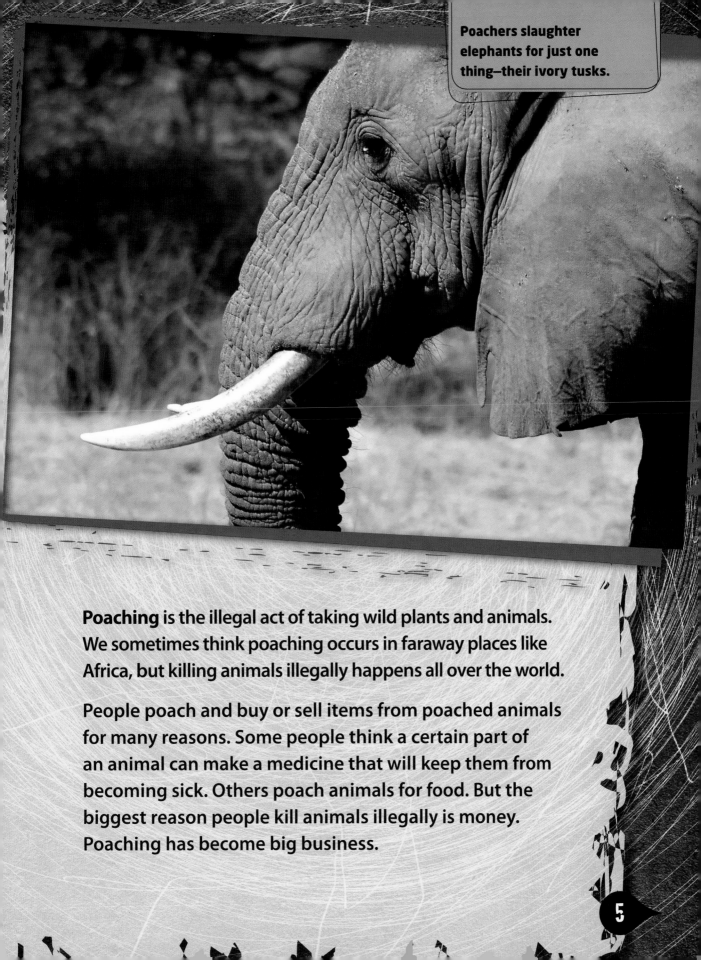

Poachers slaughter elephants for just one thing—their ivory tusks.

Poaching is the illegal act of taking wild plants and animals. We sometimes think poaching occurs in faraway places like Africa, but killing animals illegally happens all over the world.

People poach and buy or sell items from poached animals for many reasons. Some people think a certain part of an animal can make a medicine that will keep them from becoming sick. Others poach animals for food. But the biggest reason people kill animals illegally is money. Poaching has become big business.

Ways People Poach

You may already know that there are certain seasons for hunting. The fall is typically the time when it is legal to hunt deer, for example. When people hunt out of season, they are poaching.

Establishing particular hunting seasons gives pregnant animals a chance to give birth to their young. It also gives baby animals a chance to grow up before being hunted.

Poachers line up elephant tusks at an ivory market in Africa.

A mother deer cares for her newborn fawn. Both are safe—at least for now.

Just as there is a right time of year for hunting some animals, other animals cannot be hunted at all. With deer, for example, many states do not allow hunters to kill the doe—the female deer. Does give birth to baby deer called fawns and raise them as well. Protecting certain animals helps the **species** keep its overall numbers at a good level.

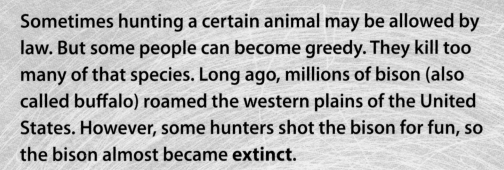

Sometimes hunting a certain animal may be allowed by law. But some people can become greedy. They kill too many of that species. Long ago, millions of bison (also called buffalo) roamed the western plains of the United States. However, some hunters shot the bison for fun, so the bison almost became **extinct**.

Passenger pigeons used to be so numerous that the sky turned dark as they flew overhead. In fact, one flock of these birds was so large that it took almost 14 hours for it to pass by! At one time, there were over 3 billion passenger pigeons alive. Unfortunately, people shot these birds for fun, and, they soon became extinct.

Bison still roam, but they were nearly all killed for sport.

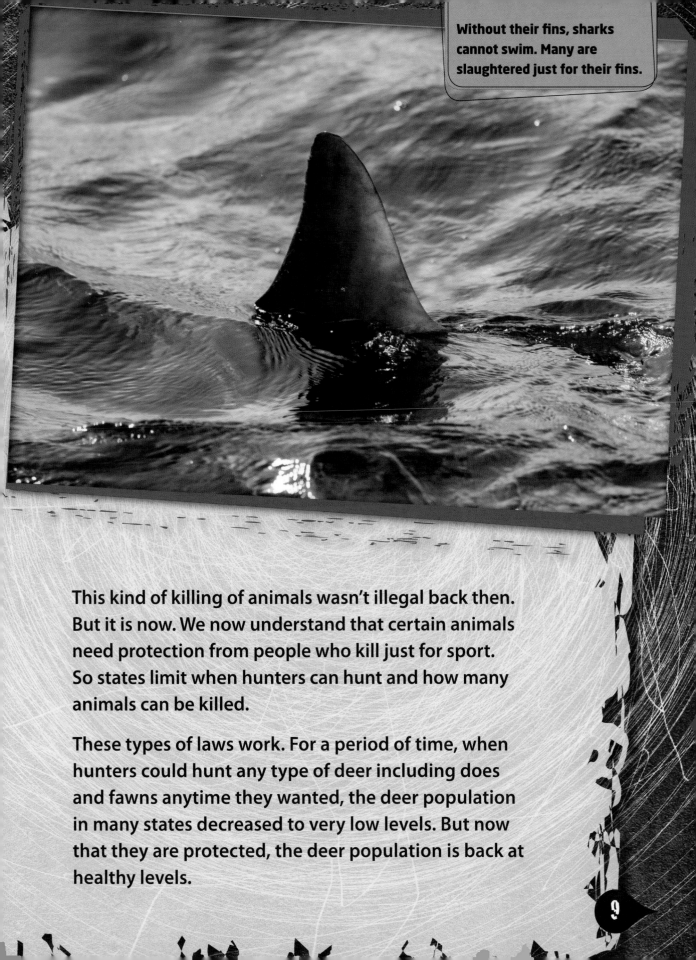

This kind of killing of animals wasn't illegal back then. But it is now. We now understand that certain animals need protection from people who kill just for sport. So states limit when hunters can hunt and how many animals can be killed.

These types of laws work. For a period of time, when hunters could hunt any type of deer including does and fawns anytime they wanted, the deer population in many states decreased to very low levels. But now that they are protected, the deer population is back at healthy levels.

One of the saddest ways in which poachers hurt animals is by hunting and killing animals that have very small numbers left in the wild. Many animals, such as elephants or tigers, are **endangered**. This means that the number of these animals in the whole world is so small that they might disappear forever. In other words, they may become extinct.

Many countries that have endangered animals work to stop poachers. They make stricter laws against poaching. They hire people to guard animals. They educate their people about how important it is not to allow endangered animals to become extinct. But laws only stop some poachers; they don't stop all poaching.

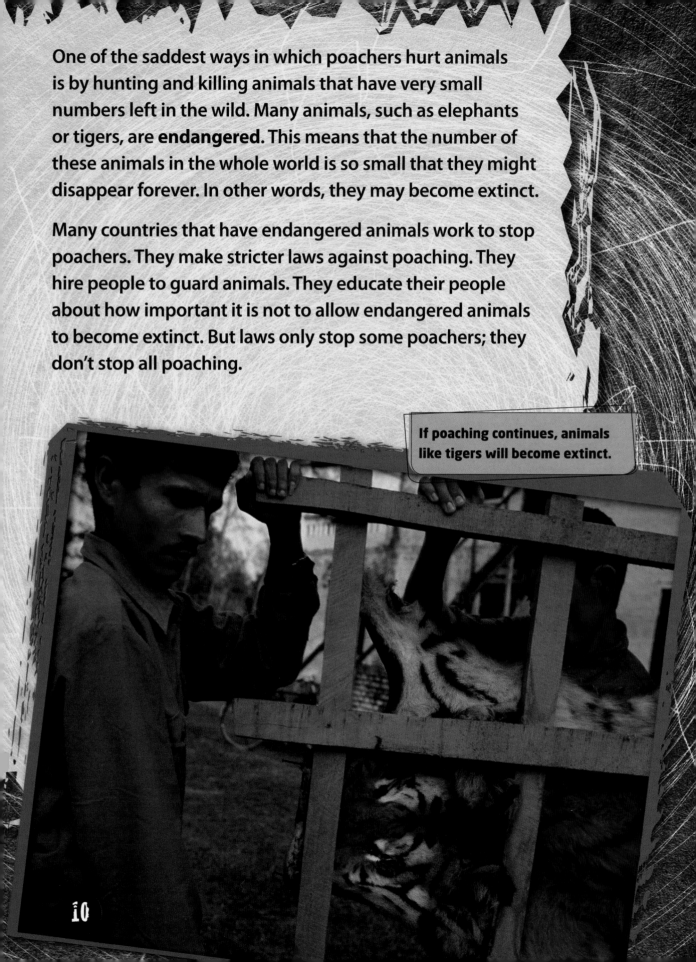

If poaching continues, animals like tigers will become extinct.

Poaching becomes a bad cycle. Poachers kill some animals that are already in danger of becoming extinct. As these animals become more rare, the demand for them becomes higher. So they are hunted even more. Poachers hunt whatever brings them the most money.

Another issue that makes poaching so harmful is that some endangered animals like rhinos, tigers, and elephants do not give birth very often. Rhinos, for example, give birth only every two to three years. Poaching even a few rhinos has terrible effects on the population of a rhino herd.

Why People Poach

Understanding why people poach is the best way to get them to stop killing animals.

One of the most common reasons that people poach is for food. You may remember stories about people like Robin Hood. He would kill the king's deer to feed the poor. This was illegal, and so he became an outlaw. The truth is that many people throughout the world do not have enough food to eat. They hunt to feed themselves and their families.

It is important to remember that not all poachers hunt and kill animals just for money.

Hungry children need to be fed. Families sometimes poach to put dinner on the table.

Farmers learn new ways to plant and harvest. When they grow more food, they poach less.

It is important to help people who do not get enough food. We can teach them better ways to farm, so they can raise more crops. We can also teach them how to raise animals that they can use as food.

Learning new ways to feed one's family is a great way to help stop poaching.

People all over the world have traditions connected to special food. For example, many families in the United States celebrate Thanksgiving by cooking a turkey. What if turkeys became endangered? Some people would still want to kill, cook, and eat a turkey even if it were against the law.

The same is true in other cultures. In some parts of Africa, it is a cultural tradition to eat **bushmeat.** To protect gorillas and chimpanzees, people who eat bushmeat must be convinced to change their traditions.

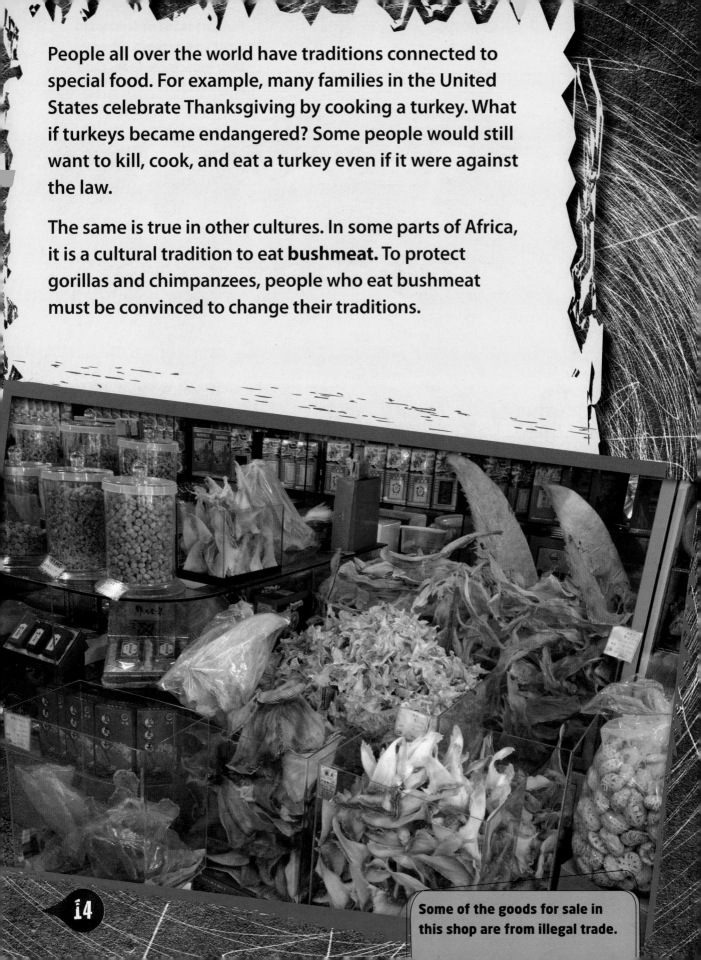

Some of the goods for sale in this shop are from illegal trade.

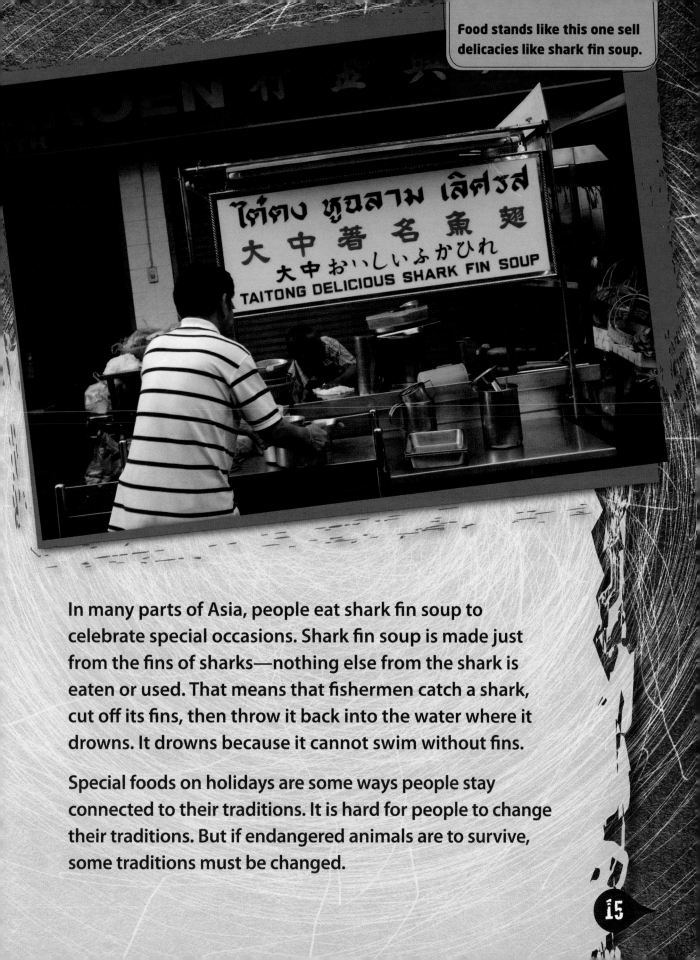

ไต่ตง หูฉลาม เลิศรส

大中著名魚翅

大中おいしいふかひれ

TAITONG DELICIOUS SHARK FIN SOUP

In many parts of Asia, people eat shark fin soup to celebrate special occasions. Shark fin soup is made just from the fins of sharks—nothing else from the shark is eaten or used. That means that fishermen catch a shark, cut off its fins, then throw it back into the water where it drowns. It drowns because it cannot swim without fins.

Special foods on holidays are some ways people stay connected to their traditions. It is hard for people to change their traditions. But if endangered animals are to survive, some traditions must be changed.

People need to be educated about the impact of their food choices, especially food made from endangered species. People can continue their traditions using different food.

Very close to the idea of traditional foods is traditional medicine. Some people think animals or certain parts of animals can make people stronger or more healthy. For example, tigers are often hunted for their meat or for their bones. Many people see that the tiger is a large, strong animal. So they think that a tiger's meat can also give a person the same kind of power. They may also believe that sick people can feel better with medicine made from a tiger's bones.

This shop in Asia sells traditional medicines made from endangered species.

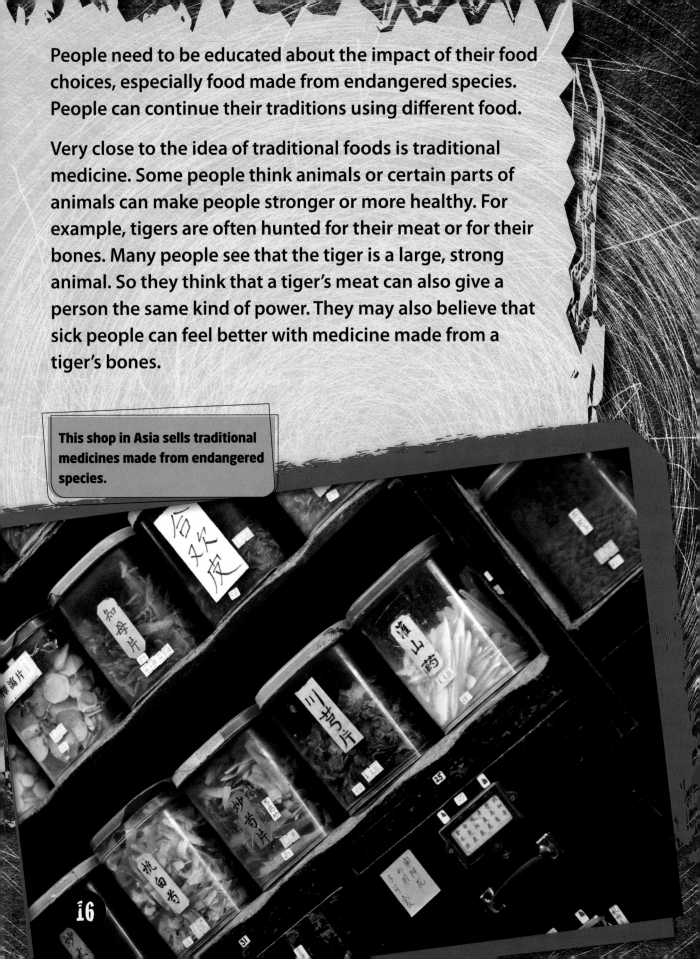

Some people think medicines made from animal parts like the ones shown here can heal them.

The slow loris is another endangered animal that is used for traditional medicine. The small furry mammal lives in the forests of Southeast Asia. The loris moves slowly and is easy for people to capture.

In some parts of Asia, people barbecue the slow loris. They think eating it that way takes away stomach pain. In other parts of Asia, pregnant women drink wine made from the bodies of three slow lorises. They believe it will make their childbirths easier.

As with traditional foods, it is very hard to get people to change their ideas about traditional medicines. People are strongly attached to traditional medicines made from animals and will go to great lengths to obtain them—even if that means hunting and killing endangered animals. But these kinds of medicines do not work the way people expect them to. Poaching an animal like a tiger for medicine is not bad just because it is ineffective medicine, it is bad because it kills an animal for no good reason.

We can, however, do something about this. We can teach people about being healthy. We can also bring them medicines that do work.

In some cultures, chicken soup is considered a cure for the common cold.

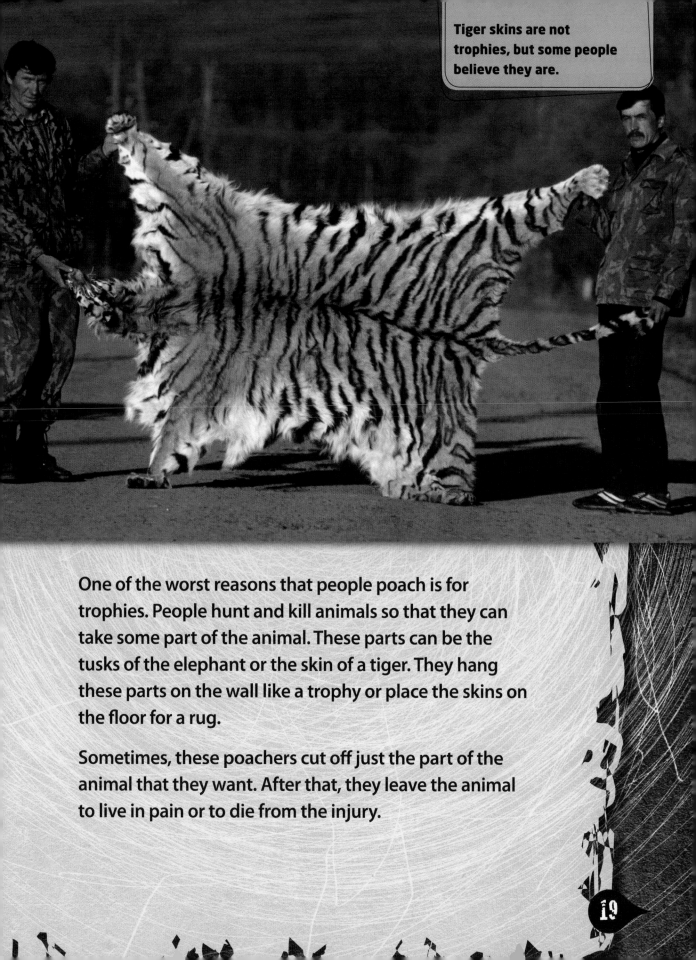

One of the worst reasons that people poach is for trophies. People hunt and kill animals so that they can take some part of the animal. These parts can be the tusks of the elephant or the skin of a tiger. They hang these parts on the wall like a trophy or place the skins on the floor for a rug.

Sometimes, these poachers cut off just the part of the animal that they want. After that, they leave the animal to live in pain or to die from the injury.

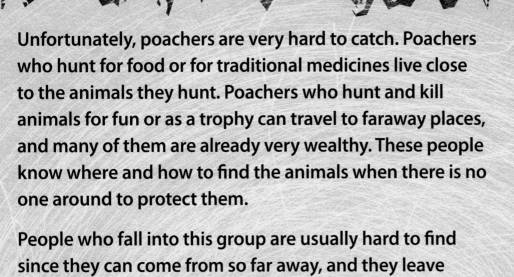

Unfortunately, poachers are very hard to catch. Poachers who hunt for food or for traditional medicines live close to the animals they hunt. Poachers who hunt and kill animals for fun or as a trophy can travel to faraway places, and many of them are already very wealthy. These people know where and how to find the animals when there is no one around to protect them.

People who fall into this group are usually hard to find since they can come from so far away, and they leave quickly after their hunting is done.

Soldiers in Africa guard rows of elephant tusks.

PRIVATE
IS HOUSE   Y

20

Where Does Poaching Take Place?

Poaching can take place nearly anywhere in the world, and it can take place at any time. We may think that poachers only hunt animals in far-off places like Africa. But illegal hunting and killing can happen in any region, on any continent.

Poaching even happens where there are already laws in place to save and protect animals. However, local customs involving foods made from endangered animals are often so important to local people that they ignore the laws. This is a growing problem in a country like China.

21

China has a huge population. In the past 30 years, more Chinese have become wealthy enough to hunt tigers. The tiger is endangered, and it is against the law to hunt them, but in China, some hunters hunt them anyway. Hunting tigers is a way to prove that one is wealthy. This means that more people are hunting fewer and fewer tigers.

The same thing can happen with traditional foods. In the past, people could have shark fin soup only once in a while because sharks were hard to catch. Modern fishing has made catching sharks much easier, so shark fin soup is now cheaper and more people can afford to make and buy it.

Shark fin soup is available even in cans.

Savannas with their wide open spaces make it easy for poachers to hunt without fear of being arrested.

Poaching is a large problem in countries with wide open spaces, like Kenya, where it is hard to protect animals. Many animals like giraffes, rhinos, and antelope thrive in vast open areas where they have plenty of room to roam for food. These vast open spaces are very hard for park rangers to patrol. These countries often do not have the money to hire people to protect the animals. This makes it even easier for poachers to hunt and kill animals.

Poaching also occurs in the oceans. It is hard to protect fish and mammals that make the oceans their home. There is just too much open water to patrol and too many miles of shoreline to watch. Poachers who hunt and kill sharks or other kinds of rare fish find it easy to poach endangered fish and mammals from the ocean without fear of getting caught.

Because animals share a **habitat**, when poachers kill one animal, they hurt many others. People think that collecting shells or coral does not hurt anything. They do not think of the many animals that use the shells and coral as homes where they find protection from **predators** and have their young.

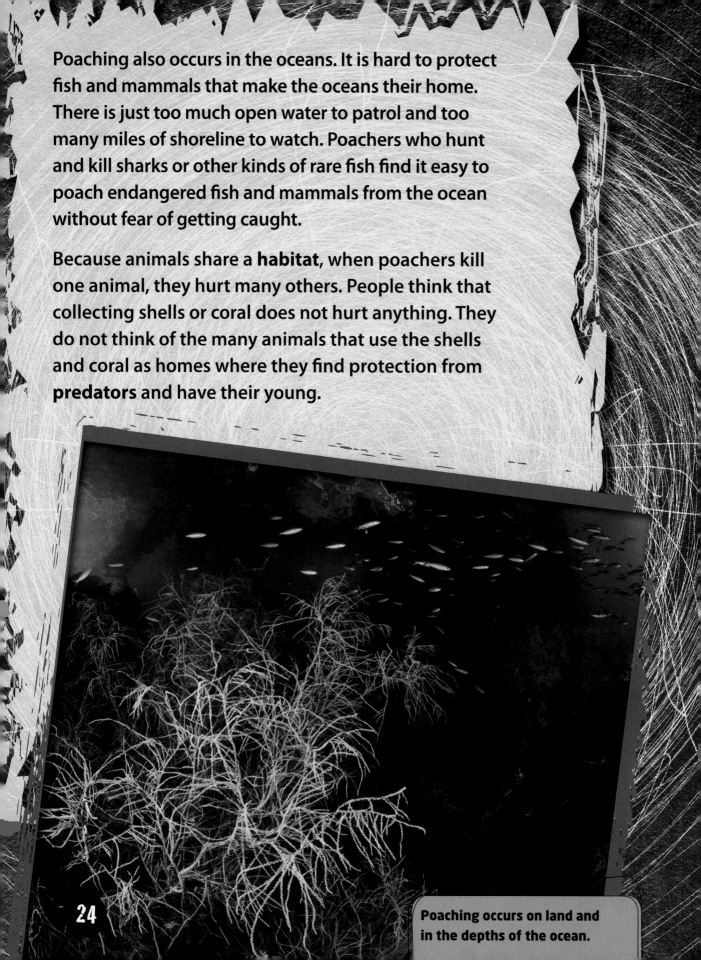

Poaching occurs on land and in the depths of the ocean.

A mother tiger moves her cub to safety.

Animals Affected by Poaching

All animals can be poached, but some animals are in more danger than others. One of the best examples of what poaching can do to animals may be the tiger.

Tigers

Tigers need a lot of space to hunt and live. But more and more people are building homes, farms, and roads in tiger territory. As an animal of prey, it is only natural that tigers see farm animals as food. So, many people who live near tigers try to kill them to protect the animals on their farms.

People and tigers being too close isn't the tiger's fault. People are crowding into the tiger's territory. People want to expand their farms or build new houses, but they do not realize they are crowding out the tigers. The tiger is simply hunting for food wherever it can find it. Sometimes that includes farm animals.

Further, the tiger is often seen as a symbol of power and strength. So tiger teeth, claws, bones, meat, and skin are worth a lot of money to people. Poachers hunt and kill tigers for these parts of its body to sell to other people. Tigers are also used to make medicines. As a result of their loss of habitat and poaching, there are only a few thousand tigers left in the world.

Tigers have few natural predators. Humans are their biggest threat.

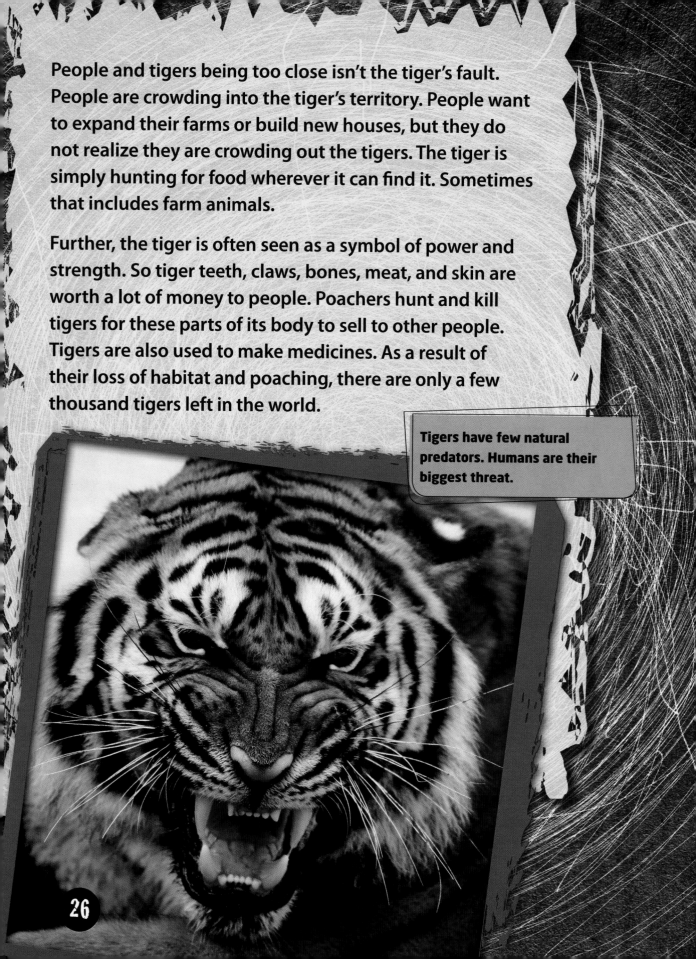

26

Although it is illegal to take elephant tusks, poachers continue to do so.

Elephants

Another sad example of poaching is the elephant. Poachers kill elephants for the ivory in their tusks. People have used ivory for hundreds of years to make piano keys and jewelry. Now, even though it is illegal to buy or sell ivory taken from African elephants, it is still in high demand. To get the ivory, poachers kill the elephant and rip out its tusks. Some poachers cut off the tusks of a living elephant, leaving it in agony.

It may seem less cruel to just cut off the tusks of a living elephant instead of killing it. However, elephants need their tusks. They use them to dig in the ground for roots to eat and to dig for water. They also use them to defend themselves or their families. So even if the poacher doesn't kill the elephant, taking its tusks makes its life much harder.

Many people around the world have stopped buying ivory jewelry. But in certain countries, especially in Asia, ivory is still in demand. So poachers continue to slaughter thousands of elephants each year just for the ivory.

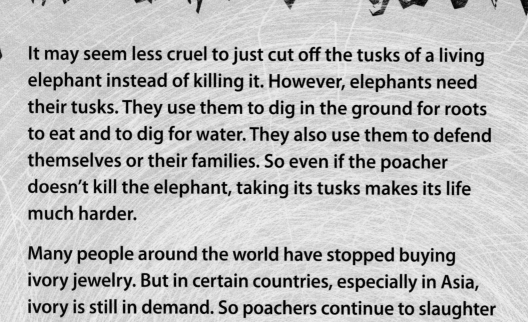

Without its tusks, an elephant cannot defend itself and may have trouble finding food.

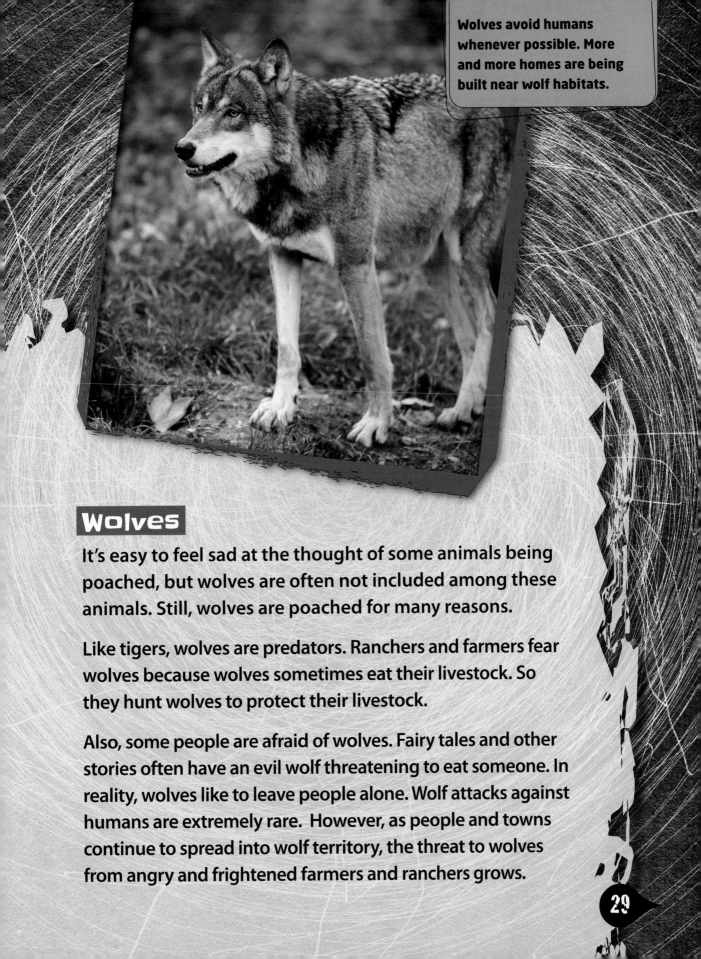

Wolves

It's easy to feel sad at the thought of some animals being poached, but wolves are often not included among these animals. Still, wolves are poached for many reasons.

Like tigers, wolves are predators. Ranchers and farmers fear wolves because wolves sometimes eat their livestock. So they hunt wolves to protect their livestock.

Also, some people are afraid of wolves. Fairy tales and other stories often have an evil wolf threatening to eat someone. In reality, wolves like to leave people alone. Wolf attacks against humans are extremely rare. However, as people and towns continue to spread into wolf territory, the threat to wolves from angry and frightened farmers and ranchers grows.

There are laws in the United States to protect wolves. Wolves have an important place in the **food chain**. Like other predators such as lions or sharks, wolves are important for keeping other animal populations down. Without wolves, deer populations can become too large. If there are too many deer, there will not be enough food for all of them. So the deer go into farmers' fields to look for food. Wolves help keep the deer herds smaller.

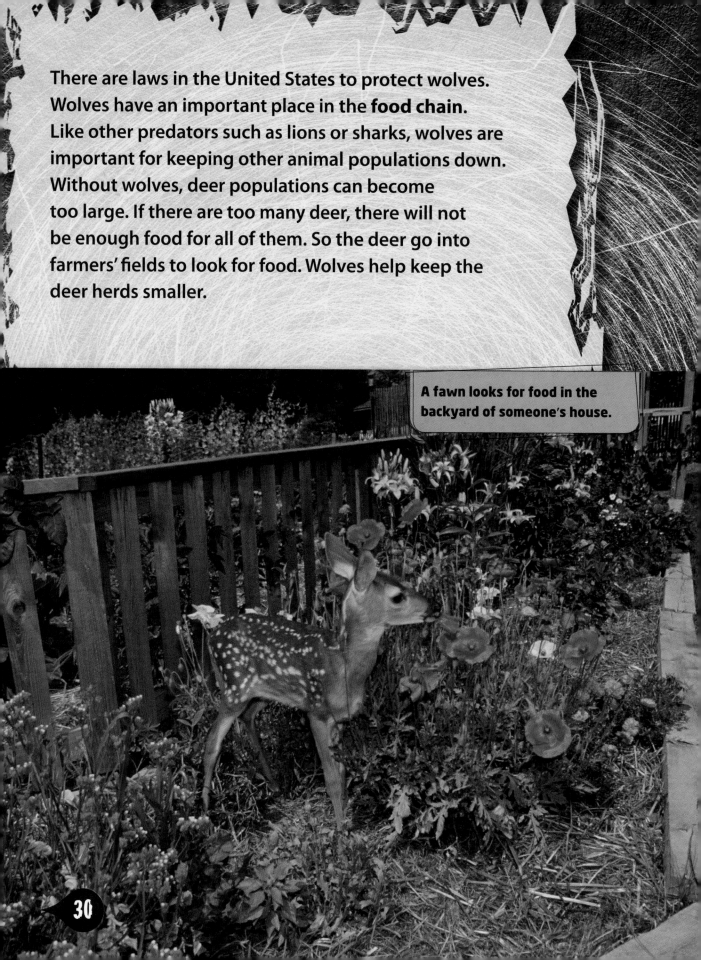

A fawn looks for food in the backyard of someone's house.

Rhinos

Like elephants and their tusks, rhinos are often hunted for their horns. These great beasts are famous for the large horn on the end of their nose. Some people use the horn of a rhino to make medicine. Hundreds of rhinos are hunted every year to make these traditional medicines. Poachers will often just cut off the horn. The rhino can bleed to death, or it dies from germs in the wound. The rhino population has decreased by 90 percent since 1970 mostly due to poaching.

Sadly, people do not know that a rhino's horn is nothing special. In fact, it is made of the same material as your fingernails!

Whales

Whales are the giants of the oceans and among the largest animals to have ever lived. But they are also in great danger from poachers. For hundreds of years, people hunted whales for oil and for food. Now we can find oil in other places, and we don't depend on whales for this resource.

Even though it is illegal by international law to hunt whales, Norway and Japan continue to poach whales. They have old ideas about whale meat and its role in their cultures. There is a reason why so many countries agreed to stop hunting whales: they are critically endangered. If we do not stop hunting them, they could go extinct. The Atlantic grey whale has in fact gone extinct.

Some native peoples still hunt whales as part of their traditional cultures.

Images of just some of the many endangered species.

Effects of Poaching

We have seen what happens when people illegally hunt one kind of animal. We need to understand the effects of poaching on other animals as well.

Poaching can lead to animals becoming endangered or even extinct. Remember the passenger pigeon? They were hunted to extinction.

Poachers do not care if an animal goes extinct. They are paid to kill certain animals and to take their valuable parts. We cannot depend on poachers to stop themselves. We have to stop them before they do permanent damage.

Illegally killing one kind of animal can hurt other animals, too. All life on this planet touches other kinds of life in some way. Plants are food for insects and other small animals. Larger animals feed on these smaller ones. This connection can be called an **ecosystem**. An ecosystem is the way in which different kinds of life use and depend upon other kinds of life to live.

So poachers who hunt one kind of plant or animal, including tiny animals like coral, are taking food and homes from other animals. People who hunt just one animal hurt many other animals. Animals depend on other animals to survive and thrive.

This diagram demonstrates how all life in an ecosystem is connected. When poachers kill one animal, the entire ecosystem is hurt.

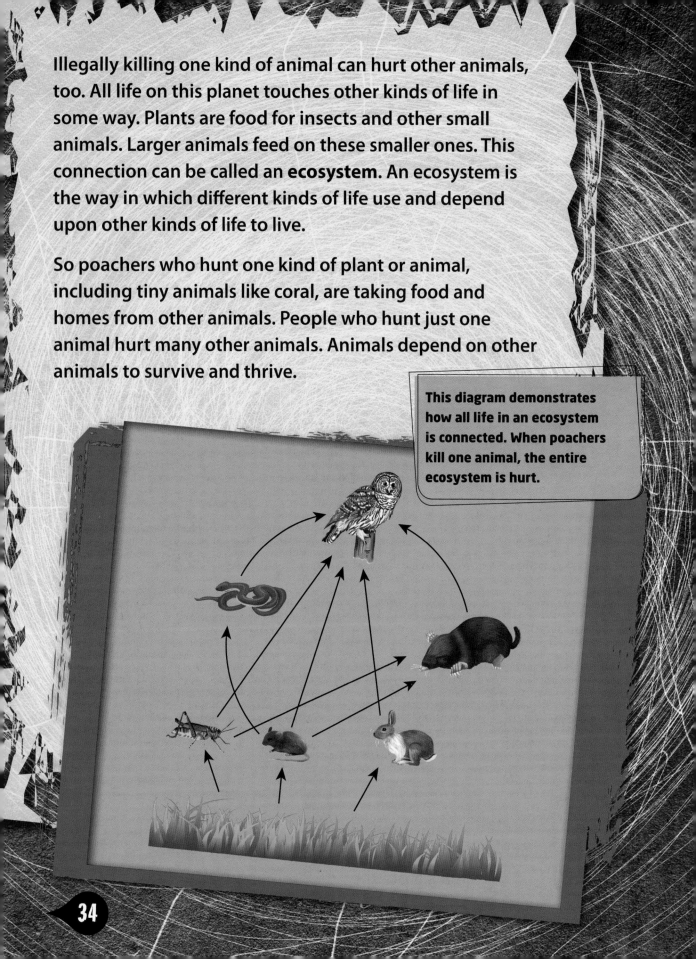

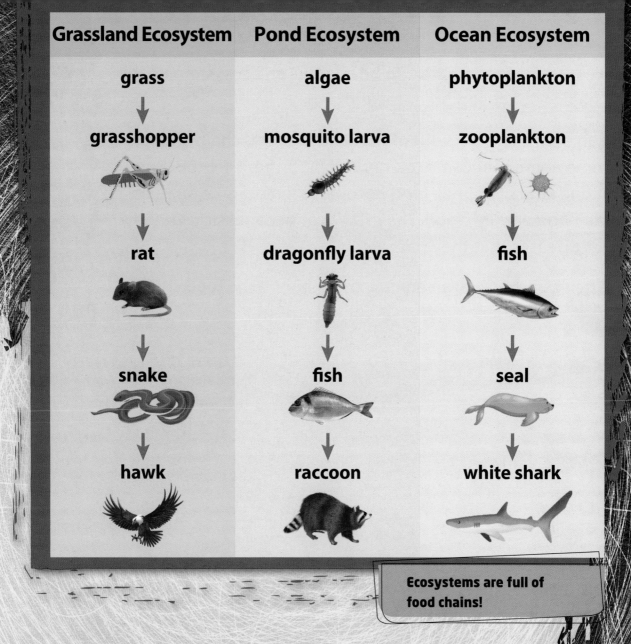

Grassland Ecosystem	Pond Ecosystem	Ocean Ecosystem
grass	algae	phytoplankton
↓	↓	↓
grasshopper	mosquito larva	zooplankton
↓	↓	↓
rat	dragonfly larva	fish
↓	↓	↓
snake	fish	seal
↓	↓	↓
hawk	raccoon	white shark

Ecosystems are full of food chains!

The way that animals eat is called the food chain. Poaching takes animals out of the food chain.

A food source like a fly is important to a spider. Without spiders, there would be too many flies and mosquitoes.

Wolves are important in the food chain, too. They keep deer populations from growing too large. If deer become too numerous, they can't find enough food, and some starve. When poachers kill wolves, they remove a predator that helps keep the deer population in balance.

Ecosystems are complex. To be healthy, an ecosystem needs a balance between predator and prey.

If an ecosystem gets out of balance, the food chain changes. Some animals become too numerous. If there are too many of one kind of animal, food becomes scarce. Some animals can't find enough food. They starve or become sick. Or they get diseases that they pass along.

When poachers kill an animal, they change the food chain.

A female lion hunts a zebra. Lions help keep the zebra populations healthy.

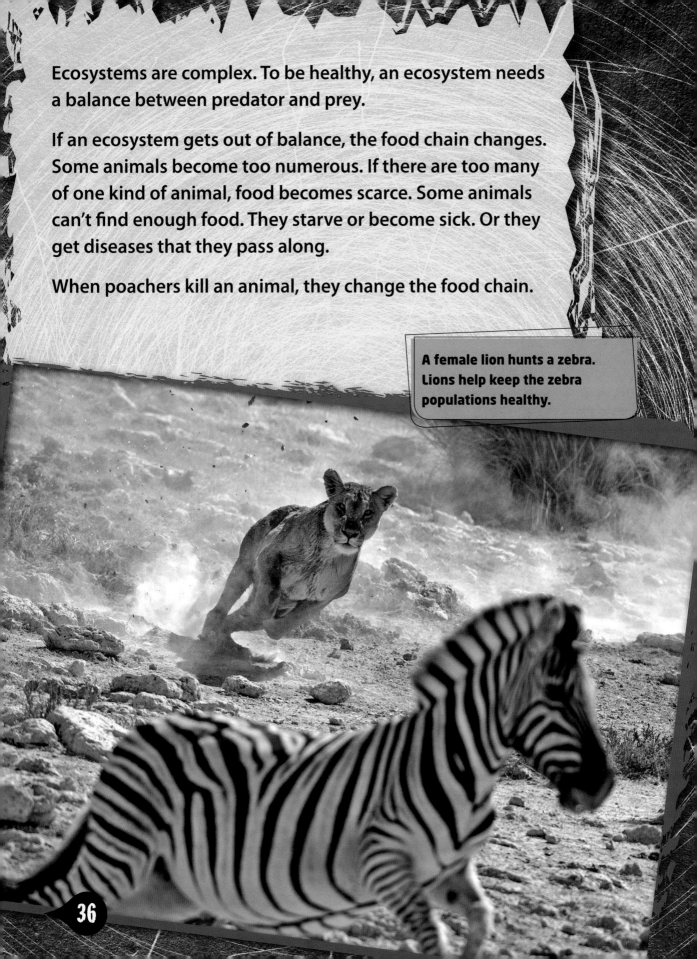

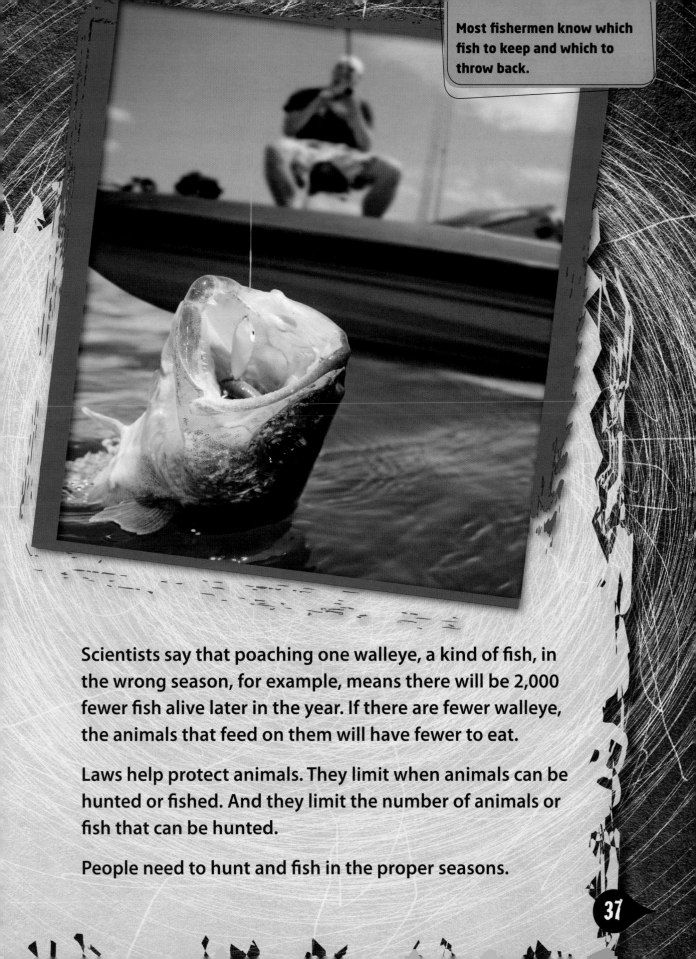

Most fishermen know which fish to keep and which to throw back.

Scientists say that poaching one walleye, a kind of fish, in the wrong season, for example, means there will be 2,000 fewer fish alive later in the year. If there are fewer walleye, the animals that feed on them will have fewer to eat.

Laws help protect animals. They limit when animals can be hunted or fished. And they limit the number of animals or fish that can be hunted.

People need to hunt and fish in the proper seasons.

Poachers sometimes hunt young animals with soft furs. Other poachers hunt eggs. Both hurt whole groups of animals. They are not only killing helpless animals, but they are also hurting other animals in that region. The eggs of a sturgeon, called caviar, are considered a delicacy and are very expensive. But taking these fish eggs means there will be thousands of fewer sturgeon born. It also means much less food for the animals that feed on them.

A healthy food chain means there is usually enough food for all.

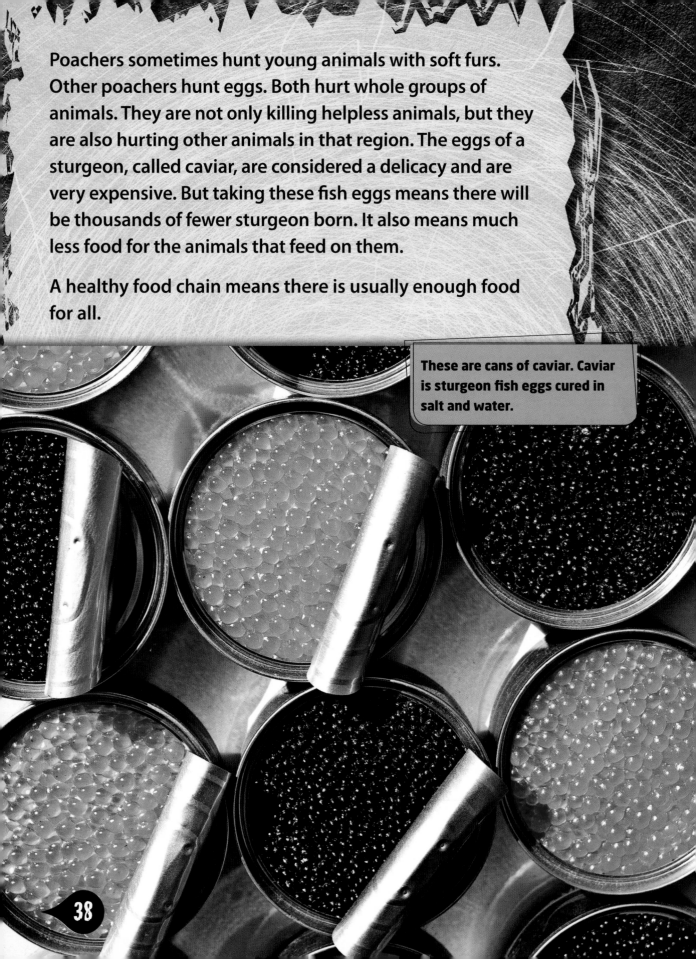

These are cans of caviar. Caviar is sturgeon fish eggs cured in salt and water.

Preventing Poaching

Poaching may seem like a problem that affects only animals in faraway places like Africa. But it affects all animals on all continents.

We all can help to prevent poaching. One thing we can do is not buy products produced from poaching. If we stop buying goods that come from illegally killed animals, such as ivory from elephants, poachers will learn that there is no money to be made from poaching.

We can also learn about products before we buy them. If any part of the item comes from illegal trade, don't buy it!

We can also not buy certain kinds of animals or exotic pets. Before you buy an animal, make sure it did not come to the United States through illegal trade. Also, make sure that it is not an **invasive species**.

Buying pets that come from very special habitats can mean that you are helping poachers. It's best to leave an animal in its own habitat.

Exotic pets are a big part of illegal animal trade. Always make sure you are not buying an animal that should not be in the United States.

Ecotourism is big business. Countries where poaching is a problem are realizing that ecotourists can be a big source of revenue.

Some countries now see that protecting animals such as elephants means that more tourists will want to visit their country. This is called ecotourism, and it helps protect endangered animals and creates jobs.

Some countries have set up large **game preserves**—areas where it is illegal to hunt. Tourists come from all over the world to see animals in their native habitats.

Other countries are tracking poachers and sending them to jail.

People who live close to endangered and commonly poached animals are learning to be good neighbors. For example, elephants can be a problem for some farmers. These huge animals can knock down fences and step on crops. They do not know what they are doing. So the farmer may become upset. He or she may hunt the elephant to stop it from doing it again.

When elephants trample crops or hurt people, some farmers turn to poachers for help.

This farmer in Kenya uses a beehive as a fence to keep elephants out.

But instead of just shooting the elephant, people are learning to live next to them.

For example, some farmers in India have learned how to keep farm animals without fences. Then, the elephants will not wreck the farm when they walk through.

Other farmers have asked scientists to figure out ways to keep elephants away. They have learned to use plants that elephants don't like to keep them away.

This is a step in the right direction. Some poaching will decrease if animals and people sharing the same space can live in harmony.

What happens if we don't fight to stop poaching? Big cats like the Bengal tiger will disappear. Massive and wonderful elephants will be found only in zoos. Grey wolves will be tracked down and killed off. Huge rhinos will be seen only in photographs. Whales, the largest creatures on Earth, will disappear forever.

There is no doubt that stopping poachers from slaughtering endangered wildlife is very difficult. We have a long and hard fight ahead of us.

Elephants and humans have worked together for thousands of years.

Poachers see animals in nature as their private bank that they can return to again and again. But nature is not about money. Nature is about the web of life that connects all things in healthy ecosystems.

When poachers slaughter an elephant for its ivory tusks, they are killing more than just one animal. They are breaking a part of the chain that connects all life together. When we harm nature, we are harming ourselves.

Alone, one voice is small. But if we join our voices together, we will become loud enough to stop poaching and illegal trade.

Glossary

bushmeat: meat taken from gorillas or chimpanzees

ecosystem: a community of living things and the surroundings in which they live

ecotourism: traveling to beautiful, natural regions that have natural or ecological interest without harming the environment

endangered: species in danger of dying out within 20 years

extinct: no longer existing

food chain: living things connected because they are each other's food

game preserves: large areas set aside for animals where it is illegal to hunt

habitat: the surroundings where animals or plants naturally live

invasive species: plants, insects, animals, or people who enter and dominate an environment

poacher: a person who illegally kills animals that are protected by law

poaching: illegally taking wild animals or plants

predators: animals that kill other animals for food

species: a single kind of living thing

For More Information

Books

Burchett, J. & S. Volger. *Wild Rescue: Poacher Peril.* Richmond, Australia: Hardie Grant Egmont, 2011.

Strom, Laura Layton. *Caught with a Catch: Poaching in Africa.* Chicago, IL: Children's Press, 2007.

Websites

African Wildlife Foundation Anti-Poaching Network
www.awf.org/content/general/detail/3583
As a subgroup of the African Wildlife Foundation, the Anti-Poaching Network works closely with local communities to educate them about poaching and to teach them the value of conservation.

International Anti-Poaching Foundation
www.iapf.org
Use this site to become more aware about international illegal poaching and trade.

Publisher's note to educators and parents: Our editors have carefully reviewed these websites to ensure that they are suitable for students. Many websites change frequently, however, and we cannot guarantee that a site's future contents will continue to meet our high standards of quality and educational value. Be advised that students should be closely supervised whenever they access the Internet.

Index